SEABIRDS

Written by Paul Sterry
Illustrated by Steve Lings

RSVP
RAINTREE
STECK-VAUGHN
PUBLISHERS
The Steck-Vaughn Company

Austin, Texas

Editor: Kim Merlino
Project Manager: Julie Klaus

Library of Congress Cataloging-in-Publication Data
Sterry, Paul.
     Seabirds / written by Paul Sterry; illustrated by Steve Lings.
        p.   cm. — (Pointers)
     Includes index.
     ISBN 0-8114-6188-2
     1. Seabirds — Juvenile literature. [1. Seabirds. 2. Birds.] I. Lings,
Steve, Ill. II. Title. III. Series.
     QL676.2.S75 1995
     598.4—dc20   93-50174
                                                 CIP
                                                 AC

Printed and bound in the United States

1 2 3 4 5 6 7 8 9 0 VH 99 98 97 96 95 94

Foreword

Seabirds can be found on all the seas and oceans of the world. This book describes 12 of the most important groups of seabirds.

The ocean is an unfriendly environment for a bird. The water is usually cold, and the surface of the ocean is often very rough. Seabirds have survived by evolving many different ways of overcoming the problems of life at sea. Many of them are buoyant and can swim and dive extremely well. Most seabirds are strong flyers and can easily cope with the worst gales and storms. A few, however, are poor flyers, and penguins cannot fly at all.

The reason why the oceans are home to so many birds is that they are rich feeding grounds. The ocean abounds with fish — the main diet for most seabirds. Some parts of the ocean are only rich in food at certain times of the year. Seabirds migrate from those areas to more plentiful feeding grounds when food is scarce.

Seabirds have to return to land for part of the year to lay eggs and rear their young. Many seabirds are awkward on the land because they are adapted to a life at sea and are more at home there.

Contents

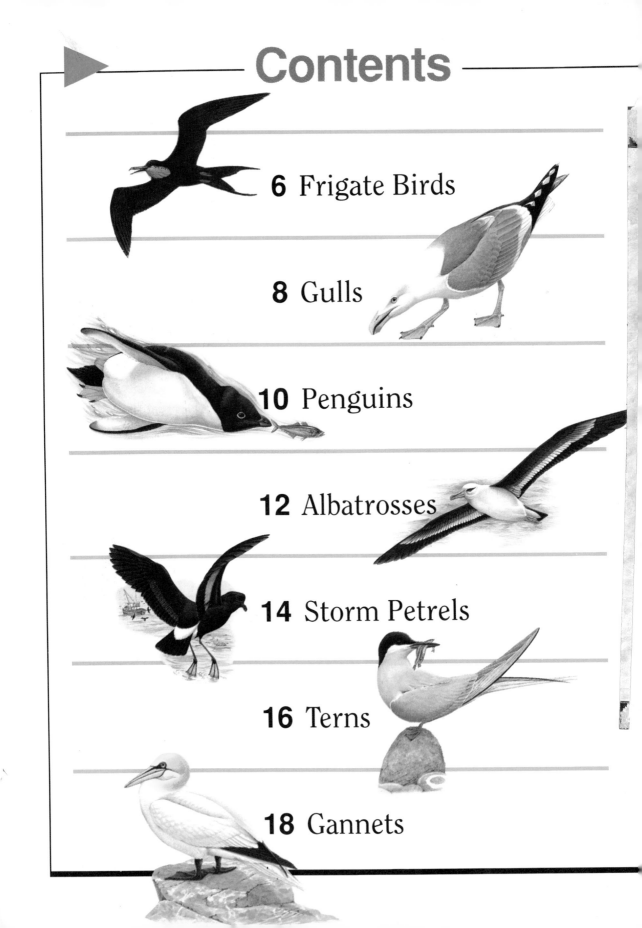

► Frigate Birds

Frigate birds are truly at home in the ocean. They roam the tropical oceans, gliding and soaring with little effort. Unlike many other seabirds, their feathers are not completely waterproof, so they cannot rest on the water. Instead, they fly for hours on end, coming to land only to roost at night or to nest. Frigate birds are also known as "man-o'-war birds" because they behave like pirates. They attack other flying birds and steal their food. There are five species of frigate birds in the world. The most widespread of these, the magnificent frigate bird, is shown here.

2 This brown booby has eaten a fish that the frigate bird wants. The frigate bird will chase it and grab the booby's tail or wings. Such an attack only ends when the booby regurgitates its fish.

▼

At the start of the breeding season, the male makes a colorful display to attract a mate. He inflates his large, red throat sac and claps his bill noisily. This takes place near the nest site.

1 Frigate birds have a wingspan of around 7–8 feet (2.1–2.4 m). The long, pointed wings are ideal for gliding without effort on sea breezes.

Brown booby

3 A frigate bird's beak is very long and has a sharp, curved tip. It is used to pick fish and scraps of food from the surface of the ocean like a pair of fine forceps. The beak is also used to attack smaller seabirds.

4 Powerful muscles enable the frigate bird to fly for hours on end. Their bones are also lightweight. In fact, a frigate bird's skeleton weighs less than its feathers!

Magnificent frigate bird

6 Frigate birds have good eyesight and can spot a flock of feeding boobies from a distance of 550 yards (500 m). They also watch other frigate birds. If one finds some feeding boobies, others are quick to follow it.

5 A flying frigate bird's long, forked tail is a splendid sight. But the tail is not just for show. By twisting it and moving it from side to side, the bird can gently alter its direction of flight.

Gulls

Gulls are such successful seabirds that different kinds are found all around the world. A few species prefer the open oceans, but most live around coasts. This is certainly true of the herring gull, shown here. These large, robust birds are often seen and heard in harbors and ports. They also live inland, nesting on rooftops in towns. Herring gulls are very adaptable seabirds. As well as catching fish and other small marine creatures, they will also scavenge on beaches. Along with other species of gulls, they can be seen visiting landfills and will even take scraps of food from garbage cans.

Herring gull

3 The herring gull's beak is powerful and has a hooked tip. This is used to tear up pieces of food and for defending itself against attackers.

2 The newly hatched chick is pale brown and fluffy. It grows quickly and, after about 10 days, has brown feathers. There are usually two or three chicks, but not all of them survive.

1 Herring gulls have a bright orange spot on the lower mandible of their beak. When the chick pecks this, the adult regurgitates food.

It takes about two years for a young ring-billed gull to look like an adult. Juveniles are brown and mottled. They molt twice in a year, looking more like an adult each time.

4 When resting, herring gulls fold their wings over their backs. The black tips overlap with the white spots clearly visible.

5 The legs of a herring gull can be bright pink. There are several other kinds of herring gulls that have different colored legs.

6 The adult herring gull has a bright, yellow eye with a dark center surrounded by an orange eye-ring. The young herring gull has dark eyes for its first year.

Ring-billed gull

Penguins

Adélie penguin

3 The legs and feet of an Adélie penguin are short and stubby, but they are extremely powerful. The webbed toes help propel the bird through the water. Sharp claws help grip the ice when walking on land.

2 Penguin feathers are more like downy fur than regular feathers. They are tightly packed together to keep water out and body heat in.

There are 16 different species of penguins, and they all live south of the equator. In fact, most are found in the oceans around Antarctica and swim in waters that are always icy. The common feature of all penguins is that they cannot fly. Instead, they use their wings to help them swim. As you can see from the Adélie penguin, shown here, the body is smooth and streamlined, so it can move through the water quickly. On land, penguins shuffle along rather slowly on their short legs. However, Adélie penguins will often slide headfirst down an icy hill to gain extra speed.

1 The Adélie penguin's wing is shaped like a flipper. They "fly" through the water with regular flicks of the wings. For short periods, they can reach speeds of 19 mph (30 kph).

▶ *King penguins nest in large colonies. After the young have hatched, they huddle together in groups called creches, looked after by adult birds.*

King penguins

4 Penguins need sharp eyes, particularly when swimming under-water and chasing fish through the murky ocean. An outer membrane protects their eyes from the freezing Antarctic waters.

6 The beak of an Adélie penguin is rather stubby. However, the edges are very rough, giving a good grip on slippery fish. The beak is also used for preening and oiling the feathers.

5 Penguins feed almost entirely on fish, which is plentiful in the Antarctic. They need all their speed and agility to catch their prey.

Albatrosses

Albatrosses are huge seabirds that live in the southern oceans, nesting in colonies on remote islands. There are 11 species in the world. The black-browed albatross, shown here, is the most common and the most widespread. Albatrosses soar and glide on outstretched wings, often in the company of ships. They hardly ever have to flap their wings and can stay in the air for days or weeks at a time. Albatrosses are very buoyant and swim high over the water. They feed on fish and marine animals on the surface of the ocean. They also gather around fishing boats and feed on dead fish and offal.

3 Albatross nostrils are tube-shaped. Special glands in the nostrils get rid of excess salt from the body. This is important because albatrosses drink a lot of salty seawater.

Black "eyebrows"

2 The beak is large and about 6 inches (15 cm) long. The hooked tip is used to pick scraps of food off the ocean, often while the bird is in flight.

Black-browed albatross

1 Albatrosses will sometimes use their legs and feet for steering in flight. Their feet are also used as brakes when coming in to land.

4 Black-browed albatrosses have a wingspan of nearly 8 feet (2.5 m). The wings are narrow and perfect for gliding over the stormy southern oceans.

5 The wandering albatross has a wingspan of nearly 11 feet (3.5 m) and breeds on remote islands in the southern oceans. For at least two years a young bird will live, eat, and sleep at sea, never returning to land.

Wandering albatross

6 The light-mantled sooty albatross is one of the smaller species with a wingspan of 6.5 feet (2 m). Like other species of albatrosses, they may live for more than 30 years and pair for life.

Light-mantled sooty albatross

13

Storm Petrels

Storm petrels are among the tiniest of all seabirds. Wilson's storm petrels are only 6.3 inches (16 cm) long and yet are perfectly at home on even the roughest oceans. They only ever come ashore to nest and breed on islands in the ocean surrounding Antarctica. Wilson's storm petrels are among the most numerous birds in the world. After the breeding season, they fly north and are found in the oceans off North America and Europe.

Wilson's storm petrels often follow fishing boats. Large flocks gather when the nets are pulled in, and the birds feed on small or injured fish.

Fishing boat

2 Leach's storm petrels have a wingspan of 19 inches (48 cm) and are fairly common in the North Atlantic. They have forked tails and clearly marked wing bars. These birds are sometimes driven ashore by severe October storms.

Wing bar

Wilson's storm petrel

Leach's storm petrel

1 Wilson's storm petrels have yellow webs between their toes. They patter their feet on the surface of the ocean. The bright color may attract potential prey.

3 Most species of storm petrels have white rumps, which are easily seen in flight. The shape of the white area can be used to tell one species from another.

4 The wings are broad, allowing them to flutter and hover over the waves while looking for food. The wingspan of a Wilson's storm petrel is 15 inches (40 cm).

Tube nostril

5 Tiny marine creatures called plankton are the main food of Wilson's storm petrels. Flocks of storm petrels are quick to spot where the feeding is good.

6 Wilson's storm petrels have long legs, which are almost useless on land. They can be seen dangling below the storm petrel's body when it is flying.

▶ Terns

Terns are elegant seabirds with long, pointed wings and graceful flight. Different species are found throughout the world's oceans, and most of them feed by plunge-diving into the sea to catch fish. The Arctic tern is a very elegant bird with plumage of soft grey and white, with long tail streamers. During their lives, Arctic terns travel farther than any other animal. They breed in northern North America and Europe then in the autumn fly south and spend the winter on the pack ice of Antarctica. Each bird flies a round-trip of about 25,000 miles (40,000 km) each year. Arctic terns may live for 10 years or more.

Arctic tern

2 The bill of an Arctic tern is blood-red and shaped like a dagger. It is used to catch fish but also to attack any intruders that threaten the nest.

1 Arctic tern eggs are olive green with dark specks. They are well camouflaged when left in the nest scrape or depression on a rocky or sandy beach.

3 Arctic terns eat mainly fish, which are caught by diving into the ocean. The male offers fish to the female during courtship. As young terns grow, they are fed larger and larger fish.

4 Arctic terns have narrow wings and a wingspan of 35 inches (90 cm). When they are at rest, the wings are folded neatly over the back with the darker wing tips projecting.

Tail streamers

5 The Caspian tern is a large species, 20 inches (53 cm) long, with an about 13-inch- (8-cm-) long beak the shape and color of a carrot.

Caspian tern

6 Sooty terns are oceangoing seabirds that spend most of their lives far out at sea. They only visit land to breed. Sooty terns nest on tropical islands. Their colonies number tens of thousands of pairs.

Sooty tern

Gannets

3 A gannet's body is strong and muscular. It can fly for hours on end and withstand the impact of hitting the ocean when diving.

2 A membrane that covers a gannet's eye acts like a pair of sunglasses. It cuts down glare so the bird can spot swimming fish.

1 The gannet's beak is shaped like a 4-inch (10-cm) dagger. The inner edges of the mandibles are rough to help keep hold of slippery fish.

Northern gannet

Gannets and boobies belong to the same family. There are nine species found around the world, and all have streamlined bodies. The gannet, shown here, is a typical member of the group. It spends much of its life far out at sea and feeds only on fish. Gannets only come ashore to nest. They are found in large colonies on islands and sea cliffs. Their nests are built of twigs, seaweed, and guano (droppings) and are spaced at regular intervals along the cliff. The distance between each nest is just slightly greater than a gannet's pecking range.

4 A gannet has long, pointed wings. At rest, these are folded over the back. The black flight feathers project from underneath the white feathers of the inner wing. Gannets keep their feathers clean and oiled.

5 A gannet chick is covered with white, fluffy down at first. After a few weeks, adult feathers appear, and the young bird starts to look more like its parents. A pair of gannets will raise one or two young each year.

▲

Gannets catch fish by plunge-diving from a height of up to 98 feet (30 m) above the ocean.

6 A gannet has large webbed feet used in swimming. They are black in color with clear blue lines on the toes.

Pelicans

Pelicans are huge birds, over 4 feet (1.2 m) long, that always live on water. Seven different species can be found, all living in warm climates. Pelicans have a huge bill beneath which is a large pouch used when catching fish. Some species live on fresh water, but the brown pelican, shown here, is a true seabird. It lives on the southern coasts of the United States and also around Central and South America. The brown pelican, with a 6.5-foot (2-m) wingspan, is the only species that feeds by diving into the water. Large groups may gather in one spot if they find a shoal of fish near the surface of the ocean.

4 The pelican produces body oils which repel water from its feathers. The feathers are waterproof, so when the pelican dives and swims, it is still buoyant.

3 The pouch is made of skin. It stretches to hold a huge amount of water and fish. When the pelican lifts its head, the water is forced out of the pouch, and the fish are quickly swallowed.

2 The bill is about 16 inches (40 cm) long. It is grayish-brown in the breeding season but dull pink at other times. The hooked tip is used as a tool when building the delicate nest.

1 The brown pelican feeds on fish. When it dives, it scoops them up into its pouch together with a large amount of seawater.

5 The plumage of an adult brown pelican is mostly gray-brown with white streaks. During the breeding season, the neck feathers are chocolate-brown and buff but otherwise are white.

American white pelican

6 American white pelicans are found around the southern coasts of the United States in the winter. They have mostly white plumage, black on the wings, and an orange bill.

Brown pelican

▶

Brown pelicans build large nests in bushes. They are made of twigs and seaweed. They breed in colonies, usually close to the ocean, and raise two or three young.

Eiders

Eiders are true sea ducks that live on the coast all year round. They are found in North America and northern Europe. Eiders have rather broad, flattened bodies and swim very buoyantly. They can also dive well and stay underwater for up to 30 seconds while searching for food. Their bodies are streamlined in the water, and their feathers are dense. During the winter months, eiders live in large flocks. They prefer rocky shores where their favorite prey—shellfish—is common. In the summer, eiders lose all their flight feathers, so for a few weeks they cannot fly until new ones have grown.

3 The female eider has beautiful, mottled brown plumage. This gives her excellent camouflage when nesting on a beach. If alarmed, the bird hides herself by pressing close to the ground.

2 The eider has a wedge-shaped bill. It is powerful enough for the bird to feed on animals such as mussels. The mussels are attached to rocks by tough threads. The eider breaks the threads and then crushes the mussel shell.

1 The female eider lays between three and five eggs in a clutch. She starts incubating them when the last one has been laid, so they all hatch together.

4 The plumage of the male eider is completely different from the female's. In flight he looks mostly black and white, but at close range his green head markings can be seen.

5 As soon as the young eiders hatch, the mother takes them to the ocean for safety. Several family groups often join together and form a creche of up to 50 young birds. They are guarded by the females.

6 The female eider has a layer of soft down under her breast feathers. She plucks these to line her nest. Eiderdown is a good insulator and helps keep the eggs warm.

Cormorants

Cormorants are large, fish-eating seabirds that live on both coasts of North America and around the shores of Europe. They swim well, using their large, webbed feet and holding their long necks upright.

Cormorants can dive for up to a minute and specialize in catching flatfish from the bottom of shallow oceans. They dive from a swimming position on the surface of the ocean rather than by plunge-diving from the air. Cormorants nest in colonies on sea cliffs and on offshore islands. In flight, they have deep, powerful wing beats and hold their heads and necks outstretched, rather like geese.

Great cormorant

3 Cormorant feathers have a metallic sheen, most noticeable in the breeding season. From some angles they are a glossy, almost purple color, but from other angles they look green.

2 Cormorants are often seen on rocks with their wings stretched out. Their feathers are not completely waterproof and have to be dried out after a few hours in the water. Cormorants have a wingspan of more than 4 feet (1.2 m), and their broad wings give them powerful flight.

White thighs in breeding season

1 Cormorants need their powerful legs to propel them through the water when they are diving. Their webbed feet are good for swimming and also for keeping the eggs safe and warm in the nest.

4 A cormorant's beak is 4 inches (10 cm) long and rough, with a hooked tip. The nostrils are partly covered, so less water can enter when the bird is underwater.

White throat in breeding season

5 A cormorant's nest is made of seaweed, twigs, and droppings. The same nest is used each year and gets bigger and more smelly each season.

6 Great cormorants usually lay between four or five eggs in a clutch. At first the eggs are pale and clean. Gradually they get stained with droppings and look very dirty. They take about three to four weeks to hatch.

Shearwaters

Different species of shearwaters can be found in all the world's oceans. The Manx shearwater, shown here, is common in the North Atlantic. This bird breeds on the East Coast of North America but otherwise roams as far away as the coasts of Great Britain and Ireland. Manx shearwaters nest on remote islands and only come ashore to their nests at night. For most of the year they live on the open seas. Like all shearwaters, they fly on wings held stiffly and are able to glide for long periods. They are usually seen in large flocks, known as rafts.

3 Shearwaters have good night vision and are excellent navigators at sea. They are thought to use the stars and sun to help them get their bearings.

Manx shearwater

2 The wings are black on top and white beneath, and span about 33 inches (84 cm). They are folded neatly over the Manx shearwater's back when they go to their nest burrows.

1 The feet and legs of a Manx shearwater are good for swimming but almost useless on land. They cannot stand upright and walk with a shuffling motion.

► *Great shearwaters breed on islands in the southern oceans. However, for about four months each year they can be found in the North Atlantic.*

Great shearwater

4 The hooked tip on the Manx shearwater's bill is used to pick small marine creatures from the surface of the ocean.

5 A young shearwater is covered in fluffy down. It takes more than two months before they are full grown and can fly.

6 Manx shearwaters nest in burrows, often ones left by rabbits. A single egg is laid on the ground at the end of the burrow.

Puffins

There are three species of puffins in the world. The common puffin, shown here, is 13 inches (33 cm) long and lives on the East Coast of North America and around the coast of northwest Europe. During the breeding season, it has striking black and white plumage and a colorful beak. In the winter, the beak becomes dull. All puffins can swim well. They catch fish by diving, using their wings to propel their bodies through the water.

Common puffins breed in colonies on offshore islands during spring and early summer. For the rest of the year they live at sea and do not come to land at all.

Common puffin

2 Puffins make nests in burrows that they dig with their beaks and feet. The tufted puffin lays a single egg at the end of the burrow, safe from marauding gulls.

3 Common puffins are fish-eaters, their favorite food being the sand eel. They can carry several fish at once in their beaks. These are brought back to the burrow to feed the chick.

Tufted puffin

1 Common puffins have short legs and webbed feet which are bright orange-red. Apart from swimming, they use them in display to one another near their nest burrows.

4 The beak is large, 1.5 inches (4 cm) long, and flat. In the summer, it is a colorful mixture of red, yellow, and blue. The birds wave their beaks to one another in display.

5 Common puffins have short, rounded wings. They fly with rapid, whirring wing beats, low over the surface of the ocean.

6 Puffins have three sharp claws on each foot. These are used for digging burrows and in fights with other burrow owners.

Glossary

Antarctica
The southernmost continent, surrounding the South Pole. A region of ice and icebergs, with oceans full of life

Arctic
The northernmost part of the globe, north of an imaginary line called the Arctic Circle. For much of the year, the Arctic is a region of pack ice and icebergs.

Bill
Another name for a bird's beak

Breeding season
The period when birds build a nest, lay eggs, and rear their young. Most seabirds nest only once a year.

Buoyant
Floating well in the water

Camouflage
Markings or coloration that help a bird hide in its surroundings

Chick
A young bird still in the nest

Clutch
The total number of eggs laid in the nest

Colony
A group of birds that come together at one site to live or breed

Courtship
The process by which a male and female bird prepare for mating and rearing their young

Creche
A gathering of young birds for protection

Display
A pattern of behavior associated with courtship and mating

Down
The fluffy feathers that cover a newly hatched young bird

Egg
An oval structure in which the young bird develops. Birds' eggs are protected by a hard shell made of calcium.

Equator
An imaginary line around the middle of the Earth, separating north from south

Eye-ring
The small feathers and skin around the eye of a bird which are sometimes brightly colored

Flock
A group of birds, usually of the same species

Hatching
The emergence of the young chick from the egg

Incubate
To keep the eggs warm in a nest. Both male and female birds may incubate the eggs.

Juvenile
A young bird that has reached a stage when it can fly

Mandible
The upper or lower half of a bird's beak

Marine
Found in the ocean

Membrane
A layer of tissue which covers and protects. Many seabirds have eyes covered by a protective membrane.

Migrate
A long, regular journey between breeding and feeding places at the same times each year

Molt
To shed feathers. A bird molts its feathers, and these are replaced by fresh, undamaged, new ones.

Navigate
To find the way. Birds have different ways of navigating on their long migrations, some of which are not clearly understood.

Nest
The site where a bird lays its eggs. Some seabirds build nests of seaweed, while others simply make a depression on the sand.

Offal
Remains of animal tissue discarded by people, such as fish guts that are thrown overboard by fishing trawlers

Pack ice
A large area of floating ice, usually in oceans by the North and South poles

Plankton
Small marine creatures that live in huge numbers near the ocean surface

Plumage
The feathers that cover a bird's body

Plunge-diving
Diving into the water from a considerable height. The speed of the dive determines how deep the bird goes.

Predator
An animal that hunts and feeds on other animals

Preen
To clean and rearrange the feathers. Some birds have preen glands which produce oil that keeps the feathers waterproof and in good condition.

Prey
The animals that are hunted by predators

Regurgitate
To bring half-digested food back up into the mouth. Some birds do this to feed their young.

Roost
To settle down for rest or sleep. Many birds roost in large groups of the same species.

Scavenge
To feed on leftover food and food debris

Scrape
A simple nest depression made in a sand or shingle beach

Skeleton
All the bones in an animal's body

Species
A group of animals that are all the same kind. They are able to breed with each other but usually not with other species.

Tropics
Warm regions of the world to the north and south of the equator

Wing bar
A marking, usually pale, running along the middle of a bird's wing

Wingspan
The distance from the tip of one wing to the tip of the other

Index